THE ADVENTURES OF
TOBIT & ANNA

a journey in wellness

by Tabitha Israel

TABLE OF CONTENTS

01

Get Rid Of The Leaven

When a friend stops by before the Feast of Unleavened Bread Tobit and Anna show him how to find the ingredients of his favorite snack

02

Discover Real Food

During dinner Tobit and Anna learn about the different types of ingredients that make up their food.

03

Digest The Facts

While at the Health Fair, Tobit and Anna learn about the digestive system.

TOBIT & ANNA

yums
BROWNIES

"Alright you two, Feast of Unleavened Bread is right around the corner and we need to get rid of all the **leaven** from the house before the **Passover**, " Mom explained.

"Think you'll find more leaven than me, sis?," Tobit asked.

"You know it! I already see some leaven in that cookie jar over there!," Anna replied as she scouted the items on the kitchen counter.

"Hey wait, I can take care of that for you Anna!..." Tobit said with a grin.

"Ha! You'll take care of it alright, right in your belly!," Anna replied as she picked up the cookie jar.

"You heard Mom, we've got to get rid of the leaven. If it's in my belly then that means we got rid of it!" Tobit said **convincingly**.

"You're right Tobit, but that does *not* mean we are going to eat *all* the leaven you find," Mom joked. "We certainly will do our best to use it all before the feast begins though. In fact, if you two find at least twelve things with leaven in it, I'll make these brownies for dessert tonight, deal?"

"Deal!" exclaimed Tobit.

"Sure, but why twelve mama?" asked Anna.

"For the TWELVE TRIBES!!" bellowed Dad as he headed to the front door.

"That's right!" said Mom.

ding
dong

"Ok, twelve it is!" Anna said, "And these cookies are **numero** uno."

"Numer - o ... what?" Tobit asked.

"Numero UNO, mi amigo! Number one!" a familiar voice said from the front hallway.

"Sammie!" yelled Tobit and Anna as they ran to greet their friend.

"Hola, mis **amigos**! Tu papa let me in. I was just stopping by to see if you all wanted to go with me to the park."

"We'd love to, but we have to get ready for Passover and the Feast of Unleavened Bread," said Tobit. "We were just counting the items with leaven and collecting them."

"Oh, that's why you all were counting. Yeah, mi mama is getting ready for the feast also. She's been getting rid of all of our snacks! I grabbed a couple of my Yumz before I left though." Sammie exclaimed.

"We know how much you love your Yumz Sammie," joked Tobit, "but you should check the ingredients to see if they have leaven."

"You know Sammie, if your Yumz have leaven in them you'll have to get rid of them before the feast starts," Anna said.

"Oh, I didn't think about that, " Sammie said.

Yumz

Yumz
"Well, you are right, but how can I check the ingredients?" Sammie asked.

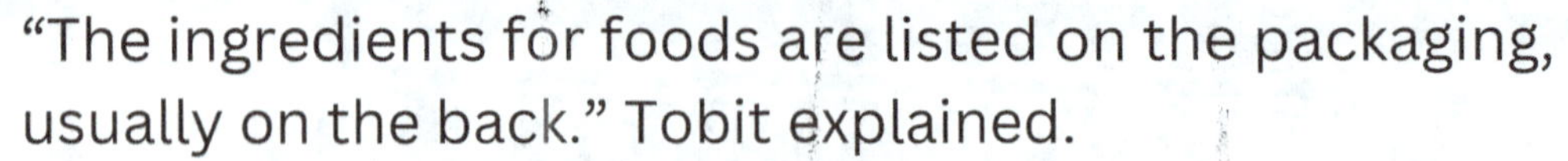

"The ingredients for foods are listed on the packaging, usually on the back." Tobit explained.

Yumz

Nutrition Facts
Serving Size = 1 cake

Calories   70
Fat   2g
Cholesterol   10mg
Sugar   16g
Carbohydrates   30g
Protein   3g

Calcium   11mg
Iron   2mg

Ingredients
sugar, flour,
water, yeast,
salted butter,
applesauce,
sweet potatoes,
strawberries,
milk chocolate,
cinnamon,
vanilla extract

made in a nut-
free facility

"But foods that aren't inside of packaging, like bananas or tomatoes, where can I find those ingredients?" Sammie asked.

"Fruits and vegetables like bananas, grapes, carrots or tomatoes only have one ingredient, so they usually don't have an ingredients list," answered Anna.

"Oh! I'm picking up what you're putting down!" Sammie said.

"Ha!" Tobit and Anna laughed.

"If you want, we can take a look at the ingredients with you Sammie," Tobit offered.

"That would be great amigos!" Sammie replied.

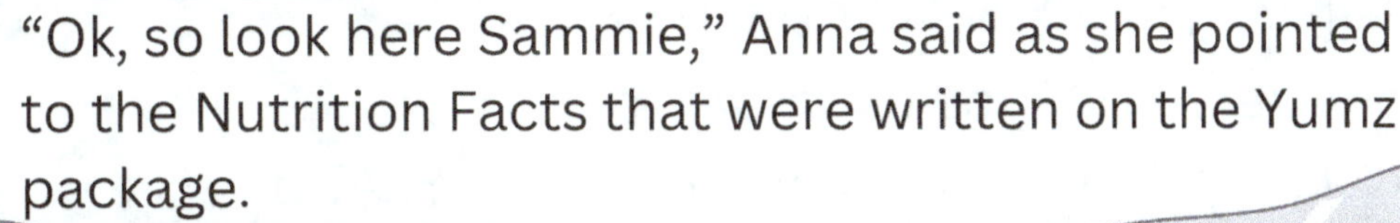

Nutrition Facts
Serving Size = 1 cake

Calories	70
Fat	2g
Cholesterol	10mg
Sugar	16g
Carbohydrates	30g
Protein	3g
Calcium	11mg
Iron	2mg

Ingredients
sugar, flour, water, yeast, salted butter, applesauce, sweet potatoes, strawberries, milk chocolate, cinnamon, vanilla extract

made in a nut-free facility

Nutrition Facts

Serving Size = 1 cake

Calories	70
Fat	2g
Cholesterol	10mg
Sugar	16g
Carbohydrates	30g
Protein	3g
Calcium	11mg
Iron	2mg

"Wow I didn't even know this stuff!" Sammie exclaimed. "But which one tells me if it has leaven or not?"

"That information my friend, is in the **ingredients,**" Tobit explained. "The ingredients tell you all the different things that are mixed together to make your food. The less ingredients the better. In this case you are looking for leaven or yeast in the ingredients of your Yumz. Do you see it?"

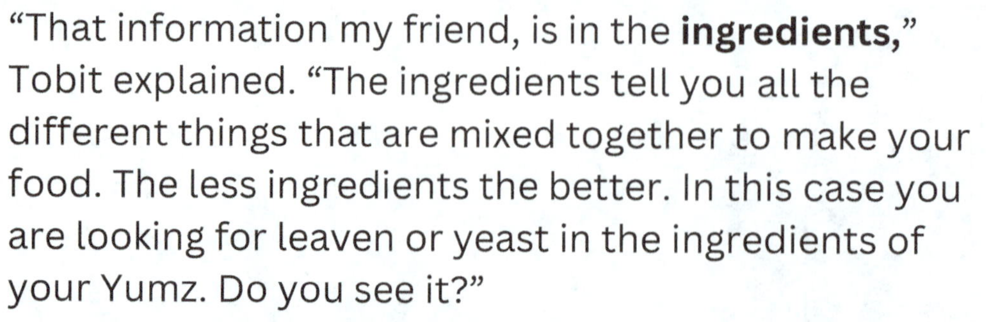

Yumz

Nutrition Facts
Serving Size = 1 cake

Calories   70
Fat   2g
Cholesterol   10mg
Sugar   16g
Carbohydrates   30g
Protein   3g

Calcium   11mg
Iron   2mg

Ingredients
sugar, flour, water, yeast, salted butter, applesauce, sweet potatoes, strawberries, milk chocolate, cinnamon, vanilla extract

made in a nut-free facility

"Si! It has yeast!" Sammie said.

"So it looks like it does not pass the test Sammie," Anna said.

"That's okay, at least now I know. Plus, that means I'll just have to eat all of the Yumz that I have before the feast starts," Sammie grinned.

"Alright Sammie, now that we helped you we need your help finding the rest of the leaven here . Are you up to it?" Tobit asked.

"Claro, amigos! Especially if I can get some of those brownies your mom was talking about!"
"Oh Sammie! Be not insatiable in any dainty thing, nor too greedy upon meats," Tobit admonished. "You don't want to eat all of your Yumz plus brownies. You'll be sick for sure!"

"Yes, this Bible verse is giving us some good advice about how we should eat and enjoy food. It's saying that we shouldn't eat too much of our favorite treats or be too greedy with our food," Dad interjected.

"Lo siento everyone. I will be mindful from now on," Sammie apologized.

"It's okay Sammie. Great job accepting correction. Now are you all ready to find this leaven? I'm looking forward to those brownies!" Dad said.

"Oh Yes!"
"Yes!"
Si, vámanos!

"Leavening agents are ingredients that make dough rise and become fluffy. Common leavening agents include: Yeast, Baking Powder, and Baking Soda."
"Sammie, Tobit and I could use as much help as possible gathering all the foods with leaven in them before the Passover begins."
"Can you help us find the items with leaven by checking the ingredients on the next pages?"

Stick of Butter

Ingredients: Cream, salt

Ice Cream (Vanilla)

Ingredients: Cream, milk, sugar, vanilla extract

Chocolate Chip Cookies

Ingredients: Flour, sugar, butter, eggs, chocolate chips, baking soda

Did You Know? When you bake cookies, you often use something called leaven to make them rise and get fluffy. Leaven is like a special ingredient that makes dough puff up.

Brownie Mix

Ingredients: Flour, sugar, cocoa powder, baking powder, salt

Loaf of Bread

Ingredients: Flour, water, yeast, salt, sugar

Cereal

Ingredients: Whole grain oats, corn starch, sugar, salt

Pancake Mix

Ingredients: Flour, sugar, baking powder, salt

Crackers

Ingredients: Flour, vegetable oil, sugar, salt, baking soda

Yogurt

Ingredients: Milk, live active cultures, sugar, fruit

Muffins (Blueberry)

Ingredients: Flour, sugar, baking powder, salt, blueberries

Pizza Dough

Ingredients: Flour, water, yeast, salt, sugar, olive oil

Biscuits

Ingredients: Flour, baking powder, salt, butter, milk

Tortilla Chips

Ingredients: Corn, vegetable oil, salt

Bagels

Ingredients: Flour, water, yeast, sugar, salt

Graham Crackers

Ingredients: Flour, sugar, honey, baking soda, salt

"Thanks for helping us out! We are excited for brownies but even more excited for the Passover and Feast of Unleavened Bread to begin."
"Si, and now I can help mi mama get ready for the feast! Hoy fue un buen día."
"Yes, it was a good day Sammie. If you want to learn more about the feast, read **Leviticus 23:6-8** in the Bible."

Admonish
To warn or reprimand someone firmly.

Amigos
Friends (in Spanish).

Convincingly
In a way that causes someone to believe something is true or real.

Ingredient
Any of the foods or substances that are combined to make a particular dish.

Interject
To say something abruptly, especially as an interruption.

Leaven / Leavening
A substance, typically yeast, that is used to make dough rise.

Numero
Number (in Spanish).

Nutrition Facts
Information about the nutritional content of a food item, usually found on the packaging.

Passover
A memorial celebration of the Israelites' exodus from Egypt.

Vámanos
Let's go (in Spanish).

MATCHING

Match each vocabulary word with its definition

——————	Admonish	——————	Leaven / Leavening
——————	Amigos	——————	Numero
——————	Convincingly	——————	Nutrition Facts
——————	Ingredient	——————	Passover
——————	Interject	——————	Vámanos

A. Let's go (in Spanish)

B. To say something abruptly, especially as an interruption

C. Any of the foods or substances that are combined to make a particular dish

D. Friends (in Spanish)

E. A substance, typically yeast, that is used to make dough rise

F. Number (in Spanish)

G. Information about the nutritional content of a food item, usually found on the packaging

H. A feast celebrating the Israelites' exodus from Egypt

I. To warn or reprimand someone firmly

J. In a way that causes someone to believe something is true or real

FILL IN THE BLANK

admonish
amigos
convincingly

ingredient
interject
leavening agent
numero

nutrition facts
Passover
Vámanos

1. The teacher had to _________ the student for talking out of turn.

2. María and Juan are best _________.

3. He spoke so _________ that everyone believed his story.

4. Flour is an important _________ in making bread.

5. It is rude to _________ while someone else is speaking.

6. Yeast is a common _________ used in baking.

7. Can you tell me the _________ of your house?

8. The _________ on the cereal box show how much sugar it contains.

9. _________ is celebrated with a special meal that includes lamb, bitter herb and unleavened bread.

10. "_________, we don't want to be late!"

WORD SEARCH

```
A D M O N I S H X R E N O M U I
C O N V I N C I N G L Y V P F N
J L X I G A N J A L E A V E N T
B F P V T A N U M E R O D I S E
E A I E G A M I G O S E D I E R
R T I M G H O C R U R L S M P J
E R N J P A S S O V E R Y G F E
T S L E S A A A E S L C T N X J C
A X I N U T R I T I O N F A C T
C I N G R E D I E N T R O J E L
T E R N D A V A M A N O S A P R
S A A S B E Q M J N L P O T M C
K L M V X L T G R I A J Z Y N E
F D F Z Q W R L D C H T B U J A
R E M O R U T I R T U N U S O P
```

Word List:

ADMONISH	LEAVEN
AMIGOS	NUMERO
CONVINCINGLY	NUTRITION FACT
INGREDIENT	PASSOVER
INTERJECT	VÁMANOS

CROSS WORD PUZZLE

Across

3. In a way that causes someone to believe something is true or real
6. A memorial feast celebrating the Israelites' exodus from Egypt
8. Information about the nutritional content of a food item, usually found on the packaging
9. Number
10. Let's go

Down

1. To warn or reprimand someone firmly
2. Friends
4. To say something abruptly, especially as an interruption
5. Any of the foods or substances that are combined to make a particular dish
7. A substance, typically yeast, that is used to make dough rise

MEMORY VERSE

Be not insatiable in any dainty thing, nor too greedy upon meats

Ecclesiasticus 37:29

King James Version Bible (Apocrypha)

dainty:

noun

something

delicious to the

taste

insatiable:

adverb

incapable of being satisfied

Writing Practice

Fill the box below with a summary of the short story, "Tobit and Anna Get Rid of the Leaven" by answering the following questions. Check each question off as you answer it in your summary. Use transition words **first**, **then** and **last** in your summary as well as complete sentences. *Hint: rewrite the question in a statement format and include the answer to the question.*

1. Who were Tobit and Anna talking to about getting ready for Passover?
2. What did Mom want Tobit and Anna to do in order to prepare for the feast?
3. Who was the friend that came to visit Tobit and Anna and what was his problem?
4. How did Tobit and Anna help Sammie find out whether his snack had leaven or not?
5. What did Tobit and Anna need help with at the end of the story?

Creative Writing

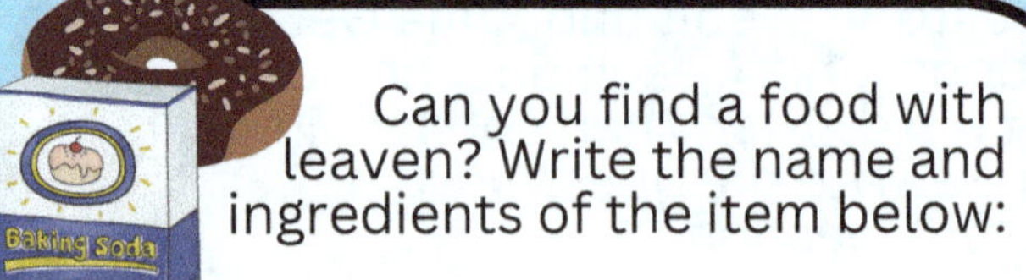

Can you find a food with leaven? Write the name and ingredients of the item below:

____
____
____
____
____
____
____

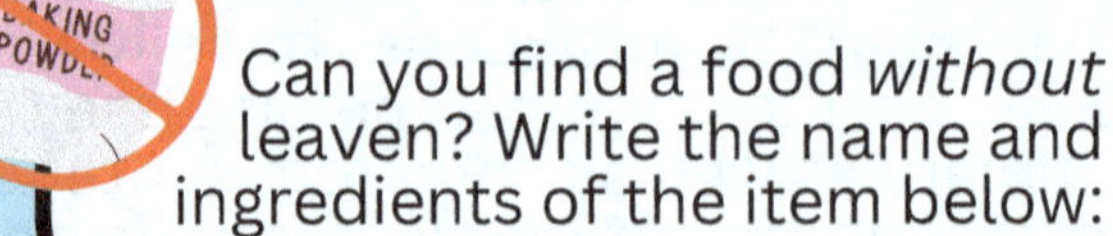

Can you find a food *without* leaven? Write the name and ingredients of the item below:

____
____
____
____
____
____
____

TOBIT & ANNA
DISCOVER REAL FOOD

"Gracias again for letting me stay for dinner. I really like spaghetti!" Sammie said.
"You're welcome Sammie, we enjoy having you," Dad replied.

"This food tastes so good Mom!" Tobit exclaimed.
"Thank you, I'm glad you like it," Mom said.
"Speaking of good food, I can't believe the Passover starts in two days! I'm looking forward to eating lamb and all the yummy unleavened breads," Anna said.

"I'm glad you said that Anna. I wanted to talk a little more about what I heard you kids talking about earlier today," Dad said.

"Are you talking about the leaven or the brownies Dad?" Tobit joked.
"Ha ha ha! No Tobit, not the brownies. I heard you say that the less ingredients a food has then the better it is. Do you know why that is?" Dad asked.

"Uh, I just remember Mom telling us that. I really don't know why though," Tobit admitted.

"It's a good practice to ask questions if you don't understand something that you are told love, otherwise you may miss out on important information," Mom said. "The reason why foods with less ingredients may be better for us is, the less that is added then, the closer the food **tends** to be to it's **natural** state," she continued.

"Well said, Mom. A lot of foods have been **modified**. Because things have been added to them like **preservatives** or chemicals, they are very different than the way the Creator created them," Dad said.
"Right! This is why mi mama grows her own vegetables in her **jardin**," Sammie said.

"I've seen your mom's garden Sammie, she's got tons of vegetables growing in it. It is **abundant** and **thriving**!" Mom stated. "I'd like to have a garden of my own some day."

"So, if a food has a lot of ingredients in it, should we not eat it?" Tobit asked.
"But wouldn't that mean we couldn't eat a lot of foods, especially the ones we like?" Sammie added.

"Well if I food has a lot of ingredients, reading them like you all showed Sammie earlier is the first step. Next you can try to learn the ingredients that are natural versus those that are synthetic," Dad explained.
Yumz BROWNIES
Yumz
Nutrition Facts
Serving Size = 1 cake
Calories 70
Fat 2g
Cholesterol 10mg
Sugar 16g
Carbohydrates 30g
Protein 3g
Calcium 11mg
Iron 2mg
Ingredients
sugar, flour, water, yeast, salted butter, applesauce, sweet potatoes, strawberries, milk chocolate, cinnamon, vanilla extract
made in a nut-free facility
"What's syn..th.tic?" the kids all asked at the same time.

"I'm glad you asked," Dad laughed. "**Synthetic ingredients** are made by people, usually in a laboratory or factory. They are often created to make food last longer, taste sweeter, or look more colorful, but they don't come directly from nature," he explained.

aspartame — Artifial sweetners make things sweet without sugar

lecithin — Emulsifiers help mix ingredients that usually don't stay mixed, like oil and water

Red 40 — Artificial colors make food look brighter and more appealing

"**Natural ingredients** come from nature. They are things you can find growing in the ground, on trees, or coming from animals. They don't go through a lot of changes before we eat them. They are usually just picked, cleaned, and sometimes cooked," Mom finished.

"Mi mama also makes a lot of our snacks because the ones from the store have stuff that I'm allergic to. When she makes them they don't have all those synthetic things," Sammie added.

"And that is a very good idea and a healthy **alternative** for sure!" Mom said.
"Mom, do you think we could make *our* own snacks? I think it would be cool!" Tobit asked.
"Yes, and I think I'd like to try to be healthier. After all, *a strong body is above infinite wealth*," Anna said.

"Absolutely! We can look at our snacks. We can even try finding replacements for ones with synthetic ingredients," Mom answered.

"Perfect, now all we need is to learn which ingredients are natural and which are synthetic," Tobit said.
"Remember, for natural ingredients we should look for ingredients that sound like real food, like 'apple,' 'oats,' or 'milk'," Anna replied.
"And for synthetic look for ingredients that sound like chemicals or hard to pronounce words, such as 'aspartame' and 'Red 40'," said Sammie.

What's In Your Food?

Use this list to check whether your food has natural ingredients.

On the next pages you will learn more about each type of ingredient, including examples.

Common Natural Ingredients

- Fruit
- Vegetables
- Whole Grains
- Nuts and Seeds
- Natural Sweeteners
- Herbs and Spices
- Dairy Products
- Meats and Fish
- Legumes
- Eggs

Fruits

apples
oranges
broccoli
tomato

Fruits and vegetables are plant-based foods that are **rich in vitamins, minerals, and fiber.** They are essential for a healthy diet and provide nutrients that help our bodies grow, heal, and function properly. Eating a variety of fruits and vegetables can help **prevent diseases and keep us strong** and energized.

A Closer Look

Fruits and vegetables are often categorized by their color groups (red, green, yellow, orange, purple, and white) because each color provides different essential nutrients. For instance, carrots are high in beta-carotene, which is important for good vision, while spinach is a great source of iron, which helps keep our blood healthy.

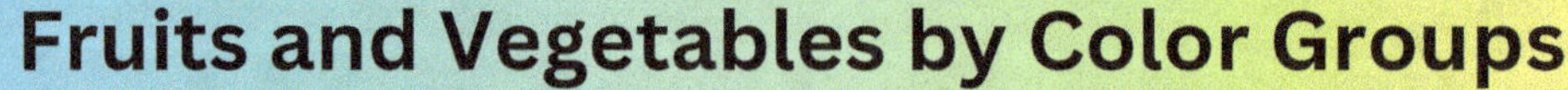

Fruits and Vegetables by Color Groups

RED

Often high in antioxidants like lycopene and anthocyanins, which can help reduce the risk of certain cancers and improve heart health.

red bell peppers

strawberries

tomatoes

GREEN

Rich in vitamins K, C, and E, as well as iron and calcium. Green vegetables often contain chlorophyll, fiber, and folate, which are essential for overall health.

spinach

broccoli

kale

Fruits and Vegetables by Color Groups

YELLOW/ORANGE

oranges
carrots
sweet potato

High in beta-carotene (which the body converts to vitamin A), important for vision and immune function. Also contains vitamin C and potassium.

PURPLE/BLUE

eggplant
purple cabbage
blueberries

Contain anthocyanins, which are powerful antioxidants that can help protect cells from damage. Also provide vitamins C and K.

WHITE/BROWN

mushrooms
cauliflower

garlic

Often contain flavonoids and allicin, which have anti-inflammatory and immune-boosting properties. Also provide potassium and fiber.

Why is it important to eat fruits and vegetables of different colors?
hint: *Think about how each color group provides different nutrients that help different parts of our bodies stay healthy.*

Which color food group could you eat if you needed more fiber?

Which food could you eat if you needed more vitamin C?

Whole

Grains

Whole grains are grains that have not been refined, meaning they still contain all parts of the grain: the bran, germ, and endosperm. They are a good source of complex carbohydrates, fiber, and essential nutrients. Whole grains help in maintaining a **healthy weight**, reducing the risk of heart disease, and keeping our **digestive system** functioning well.

A Closer Look

Whole grains are special because they are less processed and keep all their parts, which makes them super healthy for us. Here's why they are good for you: **Energy Boost**: Whole grains give you lots of energy to play, learn, and grow. They have important parts called carbohydrates that help your body stay active all day long. **Stay Full Longer**: Whole grains like oats, brown rice, and quinoa help you feel full and satisfied, so you don't get hungry too quickly. This is because they have fiber, which is good for your stomach and keeps things moving smoothly. **Healthy Heart**: Eating whole grains helps keep your heart strong and healthy. They have special nutrients that help your body stay strong and prevent diseases.

Nuts

and seeds

Nuts and seeds are small, nutrient-packed foods that are high in healthy fats, protein, vitamins, and minerals. They are excellent for brain health, heart health, and providing a quick source of energy. Including a variety of nuts and seeds in your diet can improve your overall nutritional intake

A Closer Look

Almonds are a great source of vitamin E, which is important for skin health. Sunflower seeds contain magnesium, which helps with muscle function. Chia seeds are rich in omega-3 fatty acids, which are beneficial for heart health.

Some people have food allergies, like me. This means that if they eat certain foods they may itch, feel sick or even have difficulty breathing. Allergies can even be life threatening.

Knowing whether you or a friend has a food allergy could save a life. In some cases just touching a particular food could cause an allergic reaction. Read the list of common food allergies below:

1. Peanuts
2. Tree Nuts (almonds, walnuts, cashews, etc.)
3. Milk
4. Eggs
5. Wheat
6. Soy
7. Fish
8. Shellfish (shrimp, crab, lobster, etc.)
9. Sesame
10. Gluten (not an allergy but related to celiac disease)

Natural sweeteners

Natural sweeteners are sugars that come **directly from plants.** They are often used as healthier alternatives to refined sugar because they contain some vitamins, minerals, and antioxidants. However, they should still be consumed in moderation as part of a balanced diet.

A Closer Look

Honey has antibacterial properties and is often used in home remedies for sore throats. **Maple syrup** is a good source of manganese and zinc, which support the immune system. **Agave nectar** has a lower glycemic index than regular sugar, meaning it has a less dramatic impact on blood sugar levels.

Herbs
and spices

Herbs and spices are parts of plants used to flavor food. They are often packed with nutrients and have health benefits. Herbs typically come from the leafy part of the plant, while spices can come from the seeds, bark, roots, and other parts. Using herbs and spices can make food tasty and healthy.

A Closer Look

Herbs and spices not only add flavor but also have medicinal properties. For example, **basil** is rich in vitamins A and K and has antibacterial properties. **Cinnamon** can help regulate blood sugar levels. **Turmeric** contains curcumin, which has anti-inflammatory properties and can help improve brain function.

Dairy

products

Dairy products are derived from the milk of animals, primarily cows, goats, and sheep. They are rich in calcium, protein, and other essential nutrients that are useful for **bone health**, muscle function, and overall growth.

A Closer Look

Humans began drinking cow's milk about 7,500 years ago. This started in Europe, where early farmers discovered that cows' milk could be a sustainable food source. Over time, people developed the ability to digest milk as adults.

Meat

and fish

Meat and fish are sources of **protein,** which helps build and repair tissues in our bodies. They also provide essential vitamins and minerals like iron, zinc, and B vitamins.

A Closer Look

Meat and fish have been a part of human diets for thousands of years. **Salmon** is rich in omega-3 fatty acids, which are good for heart health and brain function. **Chicken** is a lean source of protein that is versatile and can be prepared in many healthy ways. **Beef** provides iron, which is crucial for transporting oxygen in the blood.

Legumes

beans
lentils
chicpeas

Legumes are plant-based foods that are high in **protein and fiber**. They are a great source of energy and nutrients, such as iron, magnesium, and folate. Including legumes in your diet can help **keep you full** and provide important nutrients for your body.

A Closer Look

Legumes are among the oldest cultivated crops and have been a food source for thousands of years. Beans are a staple in many cuisines worldwide and are known for their ability to improve soil health by fixing nitrogen. Lentils are easy to cook and provide a high amount of protein and fiber, making them a great meat alternative.

Eggs

Eggs are a versatile and nutritious food that provides high-quality protein, vitamins, and minerals. They are especially rich in **choline**, which is important for brain health, and **vitamin D,** which supports bone health. Eggs can be cooked in many different ways, making them a popular choice for meals.

A Closer Look

Eggs have been consumed by humans for thousands of years. They are one of the most versatile ingredients in cooking, used in baking, scrambling, boiling, and more. Chicken eggs are the most commonly consumed, but quail eggs are also popular in various cuisines.

Abundant

Present in large quantities; more than enough.

Jardín (Spanish)

Garden.

Modified

Changed in form or character.

Natural

Existing in or derived from nature; not made or caused by humankind.

Natural Ingredients

Ingredients that come directly from plants, animals, or the earth and are not made in a lab.

Preservatives

Substances used to keep food from spoiling.

Synthetic

Made by chemical synthesis, especially to imitate a natural product.

Synthetic Ingredients

Ingredients made by chemical processes, often to mimic natural substances.

Tends

Usually behaves in a certain way or is likely to do something.

Thriving

Growing or developing well or vigorously.

MATCHING

Match each vocabulary word with its definition

______	Abundant	______	Preservatives
______	Jardín	______	Synthetic
______	Modified	______	Synthetic Ingredients
______	Natural	______	Tends
______	Natural Ingredients	______	Thriving

A. Usually behaves in a certain way or is likely to do something.

B. Garden (in Spanish).

C. Changed in form or character.

D. Existing in or derived from nature; not made or caused by humankind.

E. Ingredients that come directly from plants, animals, or the earth and are not made in a lab.

F. Substances used to keep food from spoiling.

G. Made by chemical synthesis, especially to imitate a natural product.

H. Ingredients made by chemical processes, often to mimic natural substances.

I. Present in large quantities; more than enough.

J. Growing or developing well or vigorously.

FILL IN THE BLANK

Abundant
Jardín
modified

Natural
Natural Ingredients
Preservatives
Synthetic

Synthetic Ingredients
Tends
Thriving

1. The apple tree in our backyard is _________ this year, producing more apples than we can eat.
2. A _________ is a place where plants, flowers, and vegetables are grown.
3. Food products often contain _________ to help them stay fresh longer.
4. The scientist _________ the plant to make it more resistant to disease.
5. _________ are found in nature and not made by humans.
6. She _________ to be very kind and helpful to everyone she meets.
7. _________ ingredients like fruits, vegetables, nuts, and seeds are packed with essential nutrients such as vitamins, minerals, and antioxidants.
8. The small business is _________, with more customers every month.
9. _________ ingredients are created through chemical processes and are not found in nature.
10. Plastic is a _________ material made to imitate natural products like wood or metal.

WORD LIST:

ABUNDANT
JARDÍN
MODIFIED
NATURAL
INGREDIENTS

PRESERVATIVES
SYNTHETIC
TENDS
THRIVING

CROSS WORD PUZZLE

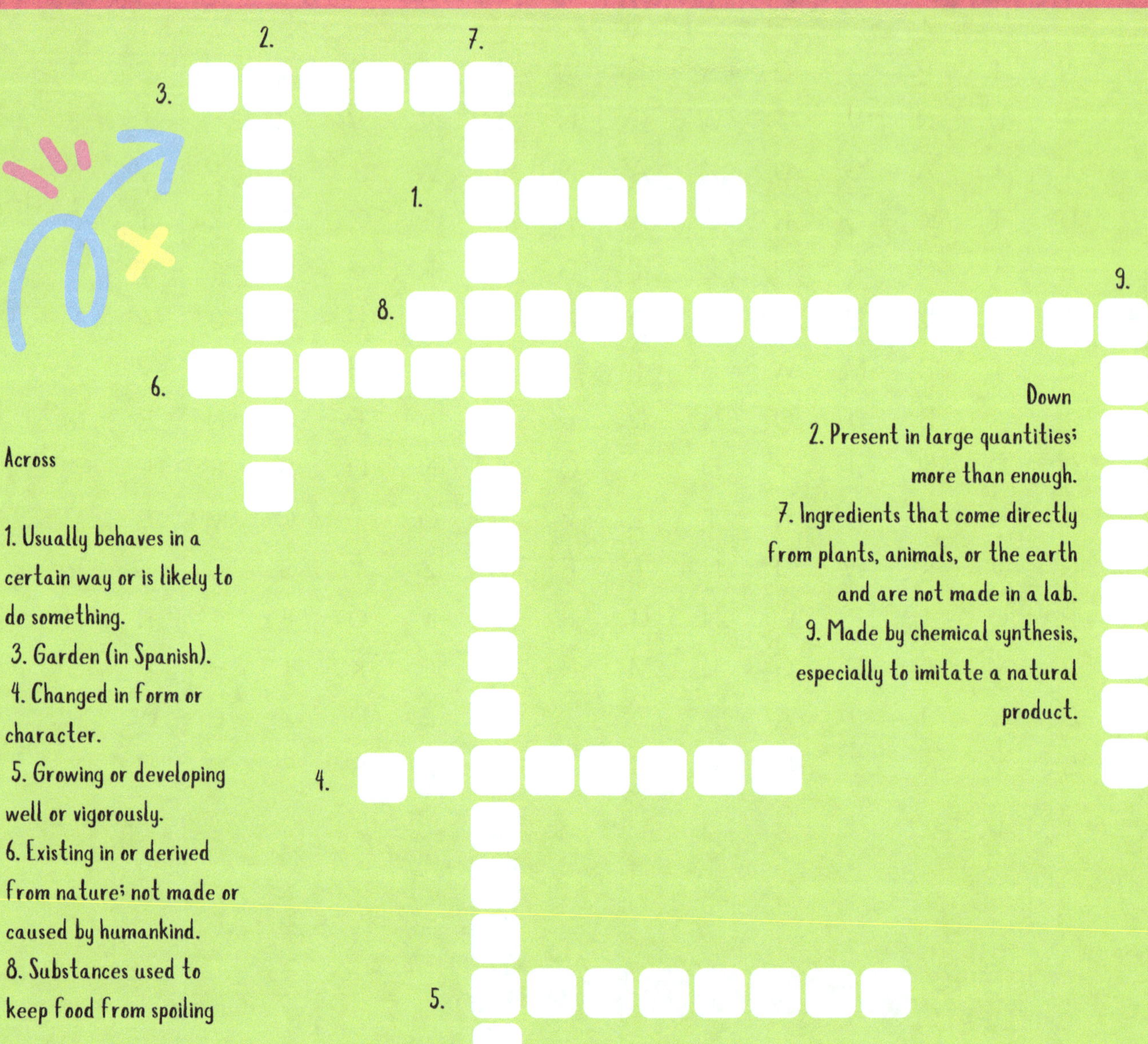

Across

1. Usually behaves in a certain way or is likely to do something.

3. Garden (in Spanish).

4. Changed in form or character.

5. Growing or developing well or vigorously.

6. Existing in or derived from nature; not made or caused by humankind.

8. Substances used to keep food from spoiling

MEMORY VERSE

Health and good estate of body are above all gold, and a strong body above infinite wealth

Ecclesiasticus 30:15

King James Version Bible (Apocrypha)

infinite

adjective

limitless or endless in size

Writing Practice

Fill the box below with a summary of the short story, "Tobit and Anna Discover Real Food" by answering the following questions. Check each question off as you answer it in your summary. Use transition words **first**, **then** and **last** in your summary as well as complete sentences. *Hint: rewrite the question in a statement format and include the answer to the question.*

1. What was everyone doing at the beginning of the story?
2. What did Dad ask Tobit?
3. Why did Mom say that less ingredients in food may be better?
4. What did Dad say makes foods different from the way the Creator created them?
5. What were the two types of ingredients that Dad said could be in food?
6. What did Mom say they could do about foods with synthetic ingredients?

Writing Practice

Creative Writing

What is one food you really like? How does it smell? How does it taste? Do you know how to make it? When do you like to eat your favorite food?

What is a food you do not like to eat? What does it taste like? What does it smell like? What do you not like about it?

HEALTH FAIR
TOBIT & ANNA
DIGEST THE FACTS

HEALTH FAIR
""Anna, check out all the booths! This looks like it's going to be fun," Tobit exclaimed.
"You're probably right Tobit, and we'll probably learn a lot." Anna replied.

"Alright, everyone. Remember to explore and ask lots of questions. This is a great **opportunity** to learn about our food, our bodies and how we can be healthier," Mom said to the group of homeschoolers.

"Look mom," Anna exclaimed, "this booth has watermelon, with seeds!!"

"I love to see it!"Mom said. "They've got seeded grapes too!"

HEALTH FAIR

"Why do you like those things Mom?" asked Tobit.

"Remember what you all learned about natural foods?" Mom began, "Well, God created our fruits and herbs to have their own seeds. I just prefer them that way."

"I'm picking up what you're putting down," Sammie replied.

"Mom, can we check out that booth with the huge pink tube in front? Please?" Tobit asked.

"Eww, I don't know about that Tobit, it looks kinda gross." Anna cried.

The Digestive System

"Aw come on Anna, it looks like a cool booth. Plus those kids leaving look like they have some sort of prize or something!" Tobit said.

"Ok, I guess I'll keep an open mind," Anna said.

"Good Day kids. Say, would any of you know why the liver applied for a job?" the man at the booth asked the students.

"Uh, no?" the kids answered, confused.

"I think he wanted to be a part of the *organ* - ization," he laughed.

The Digestive Sy

"That's just a little digestive humor for you all! Welcome to 'Journey Through the Digestive System'. I'm Dr. Digest. Are you ready to learn how our bodies process food?"
"Yes!" yelled the kids with excitement.
"Alright, let's begin our adventure! First, let's talk about what happens when we eat something delicious," Dr. Digest started. "Can you name your favorite food?" he asked Anna.

"Spaghetti!" Anna replied with a grin.

"Great choice! When you eat spaghetti, it goes into your **mouth** first. That's the beginning of the digestive system. Here, we chew up our food with our teeth and mix it with **saliva**. This helps break down the food so it's easier to swallow."

Anna replied excitedly, "So, chewing is like a mini workout for our food?"

mouth

"Exactly! Chewing is super important. Next, the food travels down the **esophagus**, which is like a slide leading to the stomach," Dr. Digest explained. "Everyone, let's all pretend we're spaghetti going down the esophagus slide!"

The kids giggled and made sliding motions with their hands.

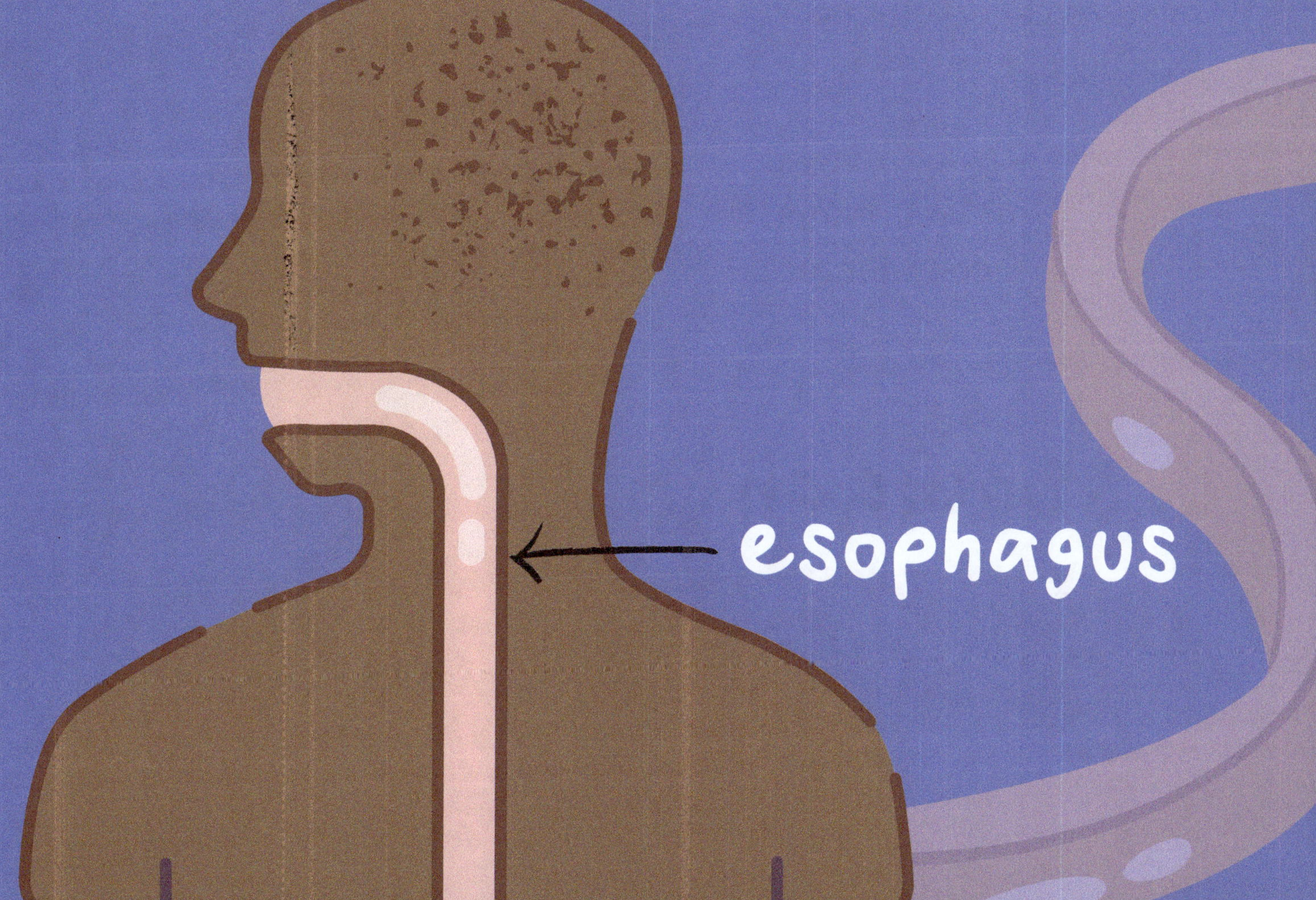

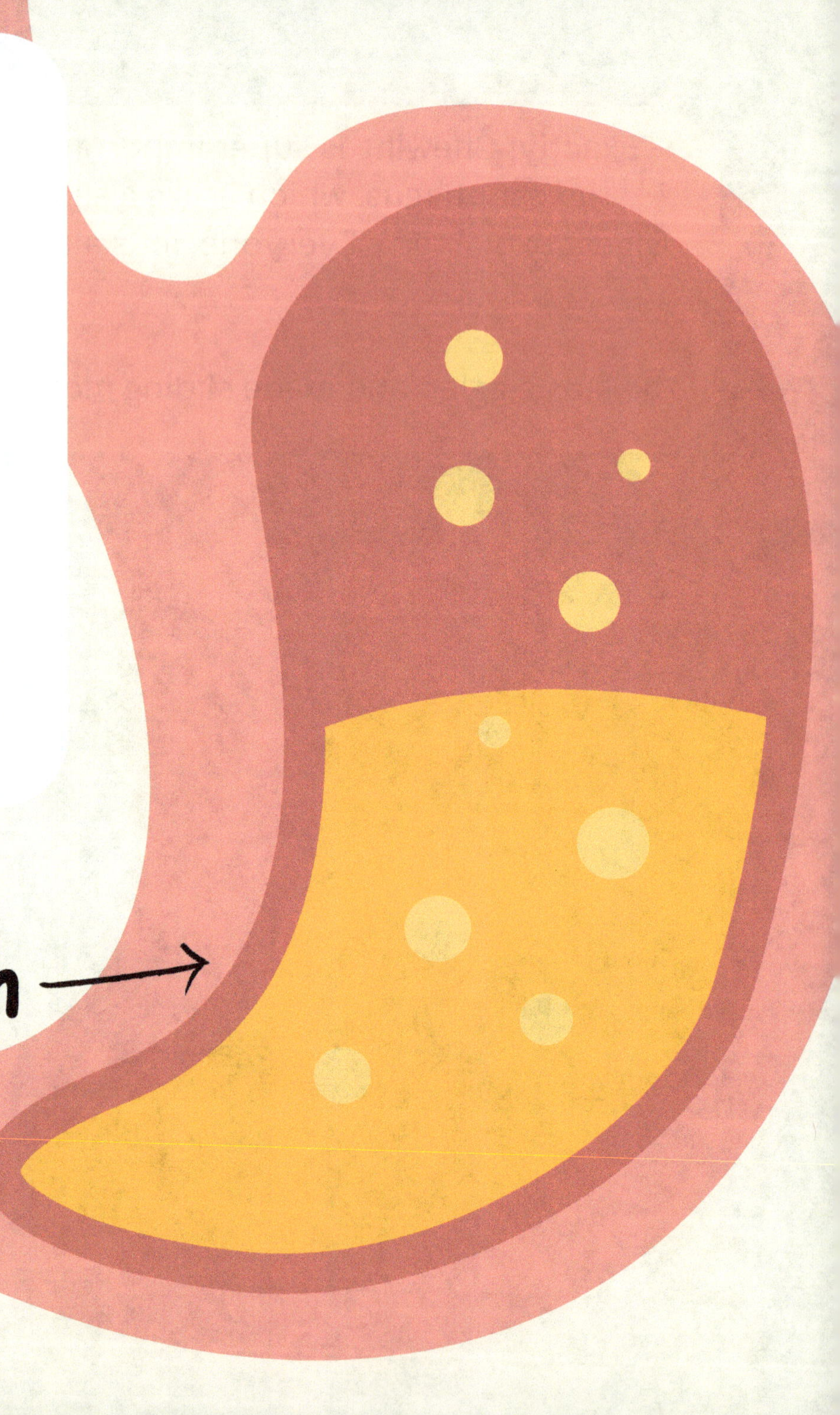

"For the next part, we enter the **stomach**. The stomach is like a stretchy bag that churns and mixes the food with stomach acid, turning it into a mushy mixture called **chyme**," Dr. Digest continued.

"That sounds kinda gross but cool," Anna commented.

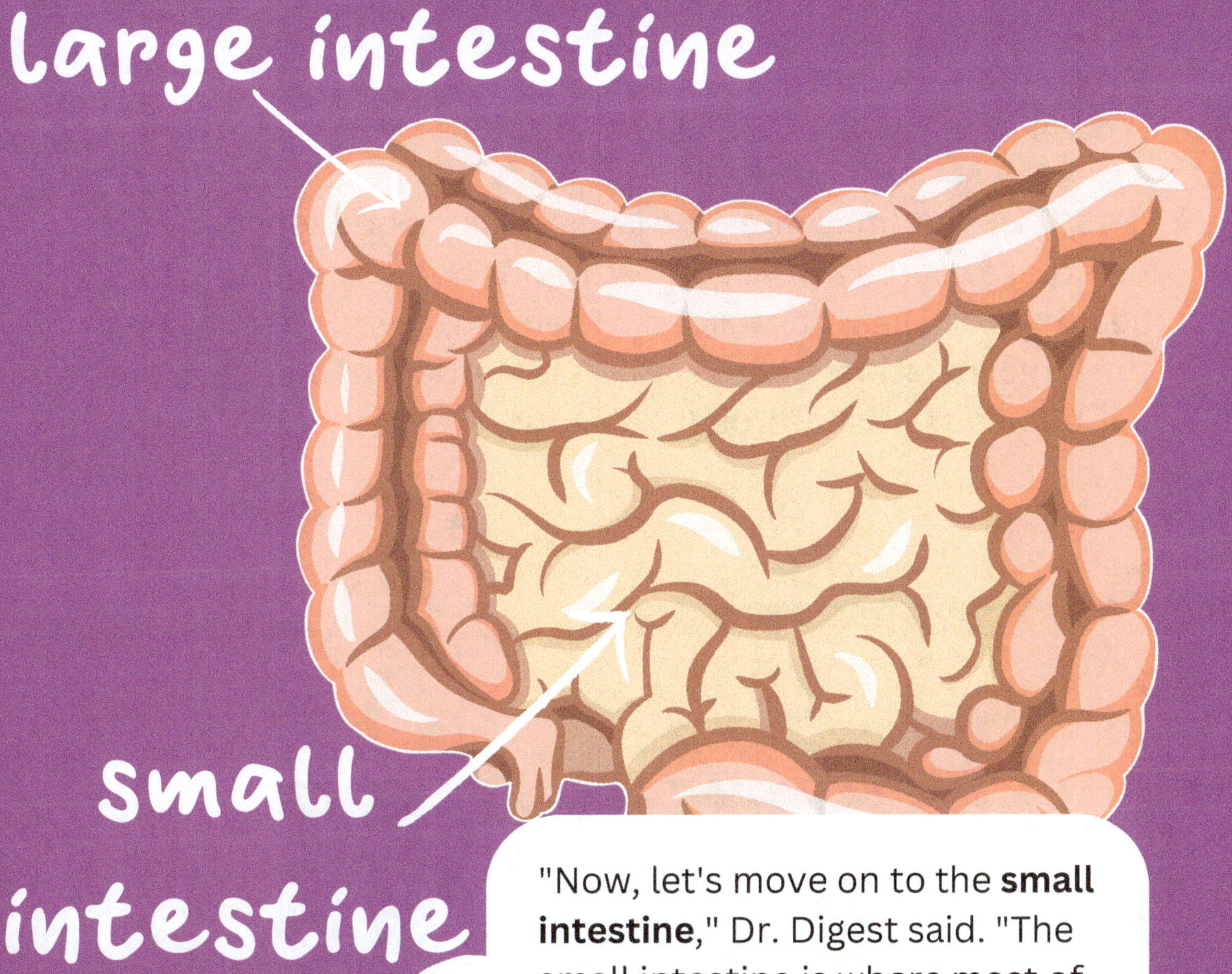

"Now, let's move on to the **small intestine**," Dr. Digest said. "The small intestine is where most of the nutrients from the food are absorbed into the body. It's really long, over 15 feet!"

"Whoa, that's longer than our classroom!" Tobit exclaimed.

"Yes, it is! The small intestine is like a super-efficient conveyor belt that absorbs all the good stuff our bodies need to stay healthy," Dr. Digest explained. "Then, whatever's left moves on to the **large intestine**, where water is absorbed, and finally, it leaves our bodies as waste through the **anus**."

"That's amazing! I didn't know our bodies did all that," Anna said, wide-eyed.

Dr. Digest nodded. "And that's just a quick overview. There's so much more to learn about our amazing digestive system."

"Ok kids, it's time for a challenge. If you can answer the next questions correctly you each will earn the 'Digestive Detective' badge. Are you up to it?" Dr. Digest asked.

"Yes!" the students all replied.

"Ok, here are the questions, " Dr. Digest began...

What is the first step in the digestive process?

a. stomach
b. mouth
c. large intestine

What is the mushy mixture created in the stomach called?

a. chyme
b. pulse
c. food

Where in the digestive process are most of the nutrients from food absorbed?

a. anus
b. esophagus
c. small intestine

What are the 6 steps of the digestive system in order?

a. stomach, mouth, large intestine, anus, esophagus, small intestine
b. mouth, esophagus, stomach, small intestine, large intestine, anus
c. small intestine, esophagus, mouth, large intestine, anus, stomach

What liquid helps break down our food so that it is easier to swallow?

a. milk
b. soda
c. saliva

Digestive
Detective
"Congratulations! See you next time!"

Opportunity

A chance for something to happen or be done.

Organ

A part of the body that has a specific function, such as the heart, liver, or lungs.

Mouth

The opening in the face where food is taken in, and where speech comes from.

Saliva

The liquid produced in the mouth that helps break down food.

Chyme

The thick, partly digested food that moves from the stomach to the small intestine.

Esophagus

The tube that connects the throat to the stomach, allowing food to pass through.

Stomach

The organ where food is broken down by acid and enzymes after being swallowed.

Small Intestine

The long, narrow tube where most digestion and absorption of nutrients take place.

Large Intestine

The wider, shorter part of the intestine that absorbs water and forms waste.

Anus

The opening at the end of the digestive system through which waste leaves the body.

MATCHING

_______ esophagus

_______ chyme

_______ mouth

_______ small intestine

_______ anus

_______ large intestine

_______ opportunity

_______ stomach

_______ organ

_______ saliva

A. The wider, shorter part of the intestine that absorbs water and forms waste.

B. The liquid produced in the mouth that helps break down food.

C. The opening at the end of the digestive system through which waste leaves the body.

D. A chance for something to happen or be done.

E. The thick, partly digested food that moves from the stomach to the small intestine.

F. The tube that connects the throat to the stomach, allowing food to pass through.

G. The organ where food is broken down by acid and enzymes after being swallowed.

H. The long, narrow tube where most digestion and absorption of nutrients take place.

I. The opening in the face where food is taken in, and where speech comes from.

J. A part of the body that has a specific function, such as the heart, liver, or lungs.

FILL IN THE BLANK

1. The ___________ is where food is broken down after being swallowed.
2. After food leaves the stomach, it turns into ___________ before moving into the intestines.
3. Your ___________ produces saliva to help break down the food you eat.
4. The ___________________ helps to absorb water and form solid waste.
5. Food travels down the _______________ from your throat to your stomach.
6. The final step in the digestive process is when waste leaves the body through the ___________.
7. Your stomach is an _____________ who's specific function is to break down food with acids and enzymes.
8. When food moves from the _________________, it goes into the large intestine
9. ___________ is produced in the mouth to help you digest your food.
10. Having a chance to try something new is called an _______________.

WORD SEARCH

```
L F B F X S N C H N F E L
J A I E B G A V H G U J Q
C Z R K O Z O L Z Y M S B
O T C G C T R C I M M H A
E P O W E I G S O V R E W
H E S O P H A G U S A R H
D K U V Y F N O P E M N C
I N T E S T I N E N L A A
T R F L W Q T K T E R U M
A A U M O U T H S H I E O
H O P P O R T U N I T Y T
O L T F V E G W U N C T S
R A O Z X J E M E I Y L A
G C R N I G M S A N Q G H
A N U S N E J K U S B L V
```

WORD LIST:

ESOPHAGUS

CHYME

MOUTH

ANUS

INTESTINE

OPPORTUNITY

STOMACH

ORGAN

SALIVA

MEMORY VERSE

And the earth brought forth grass, and herb yielding seed after his kind, and the tree yielding fruit, whose seed was in itself, after his kind: and God saw that it was good.

Genesis 1:12

King James Version Bible

- Brownie mix has leaven (baking powder).
- Loaf of bread has leaven (yeast).
- Stick of butter does not have leaven.
- Chocolate chip cookies have leaven (baking soda).
- Cereal does not have leaven.
- Ice cream (vanilla) does not have leaven.
- Pancake mix has leaven (baking powder).
- Crackers (Ritz) have leaven (baking soda).
- Yogurt does not have leaven.
- Muffins (blueberry) have leaven (baking powder).
- Pizza dough has leaven (yeast).
- Biscuits have leaven (baking powder).
- Tortilla chips do not have leaven.
- Bagels have leaven (yeast).
- Graham crackers have leaven (baking soda).

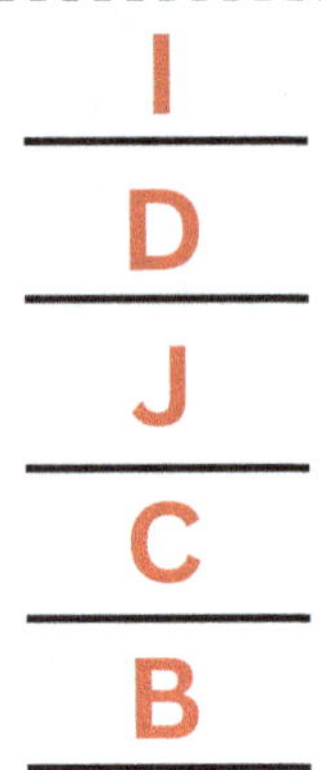

I
D
J
C
B

- ___ Admonish
- D ___ Amigos
- J ___ Convincingly
- C ___ Ingredient
- B ___ Interject

I
D
J
C
B

- ___ Leaven / Leavening
- D ___ Numero
- J ___ Nutrition Facts
- C ___ Passover
- B ___ Vámanos

A. Let's go (in Spanish)

B. To say something abruptly, especially as an interruption

C. Any of the foods or substances that are combined to make a particular dish

D. Friends (in Spanish)

E. A substance, typically yeast, that is used to make dough rise

F. Number (in Spanish)

G. Information about the nutritional content of a food item, usually found on the packaging

H. A feast celebrating the Israelites' exodus from Egypt

I. To warn or reprimand someone firmly

J. In a way that causes someone to believe something is true or real

admonish

amigos

convincingly

ingredient

interject

leavening agent

numero

nutrition facts

Passover

Vámanos

1. The teacher had to _admonish_ the student for talking out of turn.

2. María and Juan are best _amigos_.

3. He spoke so _convincingly_ that everyone believed his story.

4. Flour is an important _ingredient_ in making bread.

5. It is rude to _interject_ while someone else is speaking.

6. Yeast is a common _leavening agent_ used in baking.

7. Can you tell me the _numero_ of your house?

8. The _nutrition facts_ on the cereal box show how much sugar it contains.

9. _Passover_ is celebrated with a special meal that includes lamb, bitter herb and unleavened bread.

10. "_Vámanos_, we don't want to be late!"

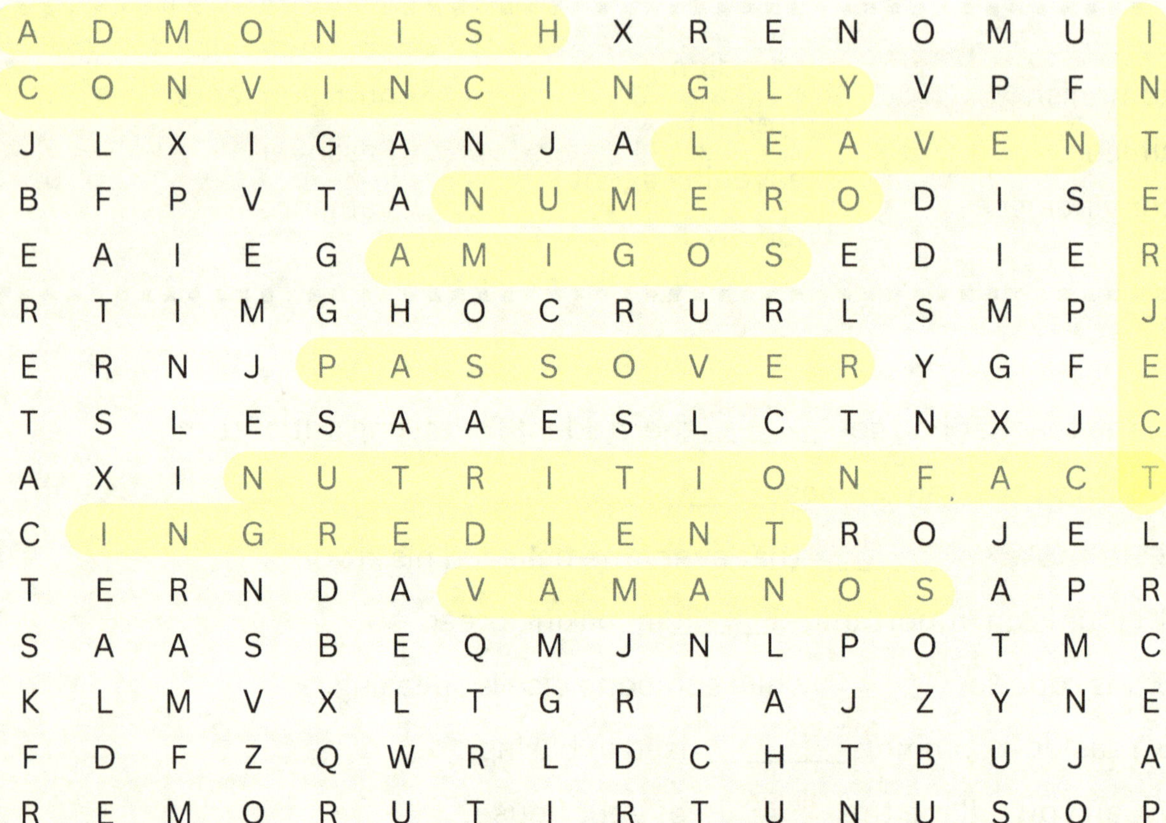

Word List:

ADMONISH
AMIGOS
CONVINCINGLY
INGREDIENT
INTERJECT

LEAVEN
NUMERO
NUTRITION FACT
PASSOVER
VÁMANOS

ANSWERS

							1.								5.		
					6.	P	A	S	S	O	V	E	R				
							D								I		
	7.						M								N		
	L				3.	C	O	N	V	I	N	C	I	N	G	L	Y
	E						N								R		
	A						I								E		
10.	V	A	M	A	N	O	S								D		
	E						H	4.							I		
	N							I							E		
			9.					N					2		N		
		8.	N	U	T	R	I	T	I	O	N	F	A	C	T	S	
			U					E					M				
			M					R					I				
			E					J					G				
			R					E					O				
			O					C					S				
								T									

Across

3. In a way that causes someone to believe something is true or real
6. A memorial feast celebrating the Israelites' exodus from Egypt
8. Information about the nutritional content of a food item, usually found on the packaging
9. Number
10. Let's go

Down

1. To warn or reprimand someone firmly
2. Friends
4. To say something abruptly, especially as an interruption
5. Any of the foods or substances that are combined to make a particular dish
7. A substance, typically yeast, that is used to make dough rise

I Abundant	**F** Preservatives
G Synthetic	**B** Jardín
C Modified	**H** Synthetic Ingredients
D Natural	**J** Tends
A Thriving	**E** Natural Ingredients

A. Usually behaves in a certain way or is likely to do something.

B. Garden (in Spanish).

C. Changed in form or character.

D. Existing in or derived from nature; not made or caused by humankind.

E. Ingredients that come directly from plants, animals, or the earth and are not made in a lab.

F. Substances used to keep food from spoiling.

G. Made by chemical synthesis, especially to imitate a natural product.

H. Ingredients made by chemical processes, often to mimic natural substances.

I. Present in large quantities; more than enough.

J. Growing or developing well or vigorously.

Abundant
Jardín
modified

Natural
Natural Ingredients
Preservatives
Synthetic

Synthetic Ingredients
Tends
Thriving

1. The apple tree in our backyard is __abundant__ this year, producing more apples than we can eat.
2. A __jardin__ is a place where plants, flowers, and vegetables are grown.
3. Food products often contain __preservatives__ to help them stay fresh longer.
4. The scientist __modified__ the plant to make it more resistant to disease.
5. __Natural ingredients__ are found in nature and not made by humans.
6. She __tends__ to be very kind and helpful to everyone she meets.
7. __Natural__ ingredients like fruits, vegetables, nuts, and seeds are packed with essential nutrients such as vitamins, minerals, and antioxidants.
8. The small business is __thriving__, with more customers every month.
9. __Synthetic ingredients__ ingredients are created through chemical processes and are not found in nature.
10. Plastic is a __synthetic__ material made to imitate natural products like wood or metal.

WORD LIST:

ABUNDANT
JARDÍN
MODIFIED
NATURAL
INGREDIENTS

PRESERVATIVES
SYNTHETIC
TENDS
THRIVING

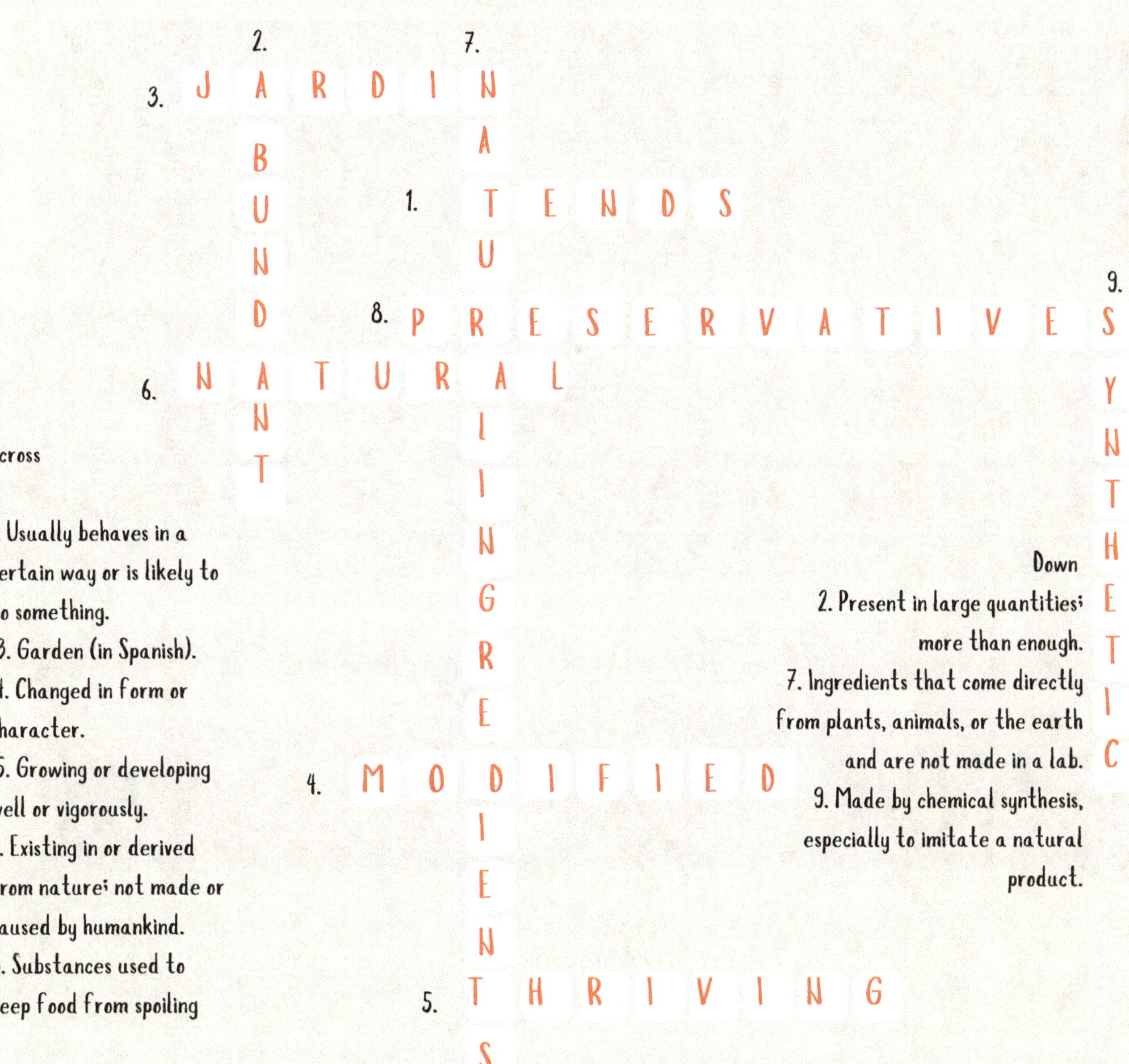

Across

1. Usually behaves in a certain way or is likely to do something.
3. Garden (in Spanish).
4. Changed in form or character.
5. Growing or developing well or vigorously.
6. Existing in or derived from nature; not made or caused by humankind.
8. Substances used to keep food from spoiling

What is the first step in the digestive process?

a. stomach
b. mouth
c. large intestine

What is the mushy mixture created in the stomach called?

a. chyme
b. pulse
c. food

Where in the digestive process are most of the nutrients from food absorbed?

a. anus
b. esophagus
c. small intestine

What are the 6 steps of the digestive system in order?

a. stomach, mouth, large intestine, anus, esophagus, small intestine

b. mouth, esophagus, stomach, small intestine, large intestine, anus

c. small intestine, esophagus, mouth, large intestine, anus, stomach

What liquid helps break down our food so that it is easier to swallow?

a. milk

b. soda

c. saliva

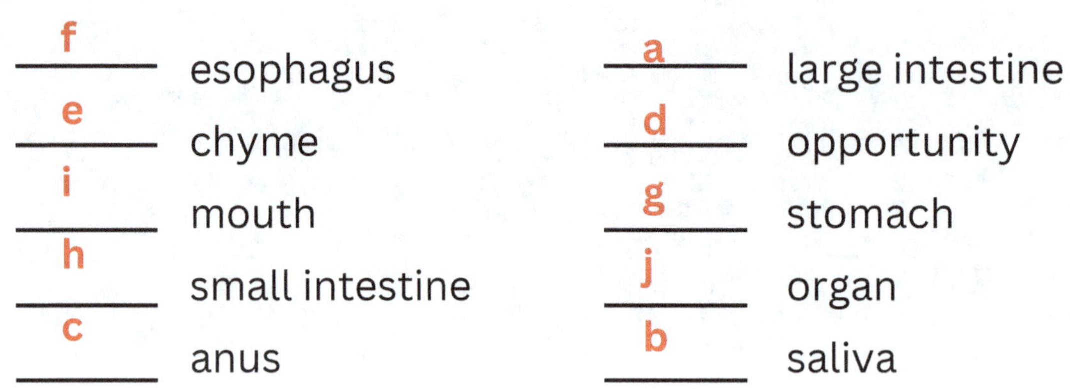

f esophagus	**a** large intestine	
e chyme	**d** opportunity	
i mouth	**g** stomach	
h small intestine	**j** organ	
c anus	**b** saliva	

A. The wider, shorter part of the intestine that absorbs water and forms waste.

B. The liquid produced in the mouth that helps break down food.

C. The opening at the end of the digestive system through which waste leaves the body.

D. A chance for something to happen or be done.

E. The thick, partly digested food that moves from the stomach to the small intestine.

F. The tube that connects the throat to the stomach, allowing food to pass through.

G. The organ where food is broken down by acid and enzymes after being swallowed.

H. The long, narrow tube where most digestion and absorption of nutrients take place.

I. The opening in the face where food is taken in, and where speech comes from.

J. A part of the body that has a specific function, such as the heart, liver, or lungs.

esophagus   anus   organ

chyme   large intestine   Saliva

mouth   opportunity

small intestine   stomach

1. The **stomach** __________ is where food is broken down after being swallowed.
2. After food leaves the stomach, it turns into **chyme** _______ before moving into the intestines.
3. Your **mouth** _______ produces saliva to help break down the food you eat.
4. The **large intestine** _____________ helps to absorb water and form solid waste.
5. Food travels down the **esophagus** __________ from your throat to your stomach.
6. The final step in the digestive process is when waste leaves the body through the **anus** _________.
7. Your stomach is an **organ** __________ who's specific function is to break down food with acids and enzymes.
8. When food moves from the **small intestine** ____________, it goes into the large intestine
9. **Saliva** _______ is produced in the mouth to help you digest your food.
10. Having a chance to try something new is called an **opportunity** ___________.

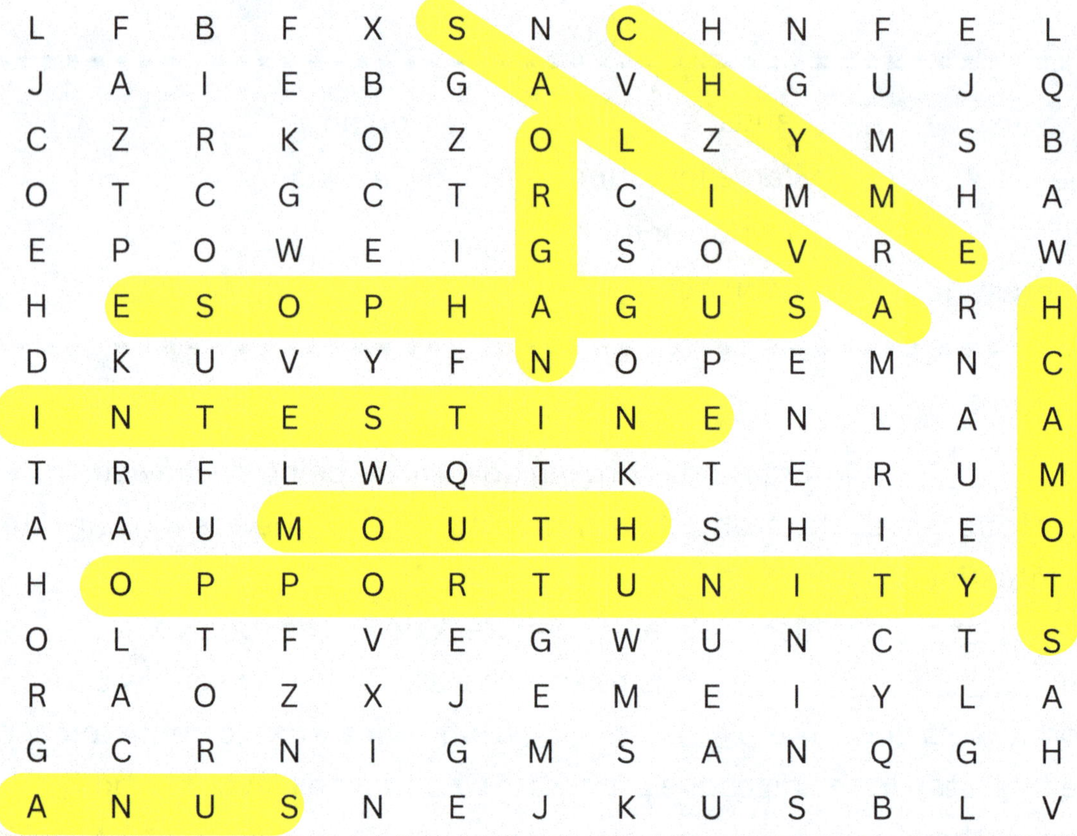

WORD LIST:

ESOPHAGUS
CHYME
MOUTH
ANUS

INTESTINE
OPPORTUNITY
STOMACH
ORGAN
SALIVA

Thank You for Purchasing
"The Adventures of Tobit and Anna: A Journey In Wellness"!

We hope you enjoyed this book. If you did, be sure to visit the Imagery Store at **www.imagerymatters.org** for more educational items that costs less than $1!

Have You Heard of COE?

We've designed an innovative space to learn and excel inside the Children of Excellence Learning Space (COE). Inside COE, students have access to live classes that cover topics like wellness, innovation, STEM, and the Bible in addition to, a large and growing library of resources to explore history, careers, science, math and more!

If your student loved this book, they are bound to find something exciting within COE. Designed for ages 7+, COE integrates representation and the Bible into every lesson, providing a rich, meaningful educational experience.
Find out more by scanning the QR code below!

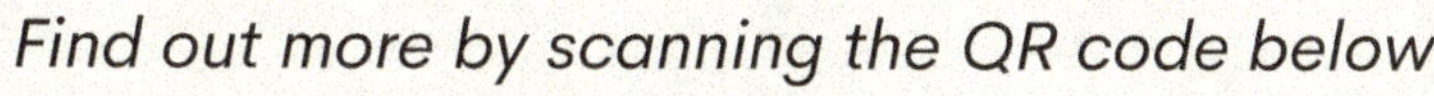

www.ingramcontent.com/pod-product-compliance
Lightning Source LLC
Chambersburg PA
CBHW081941160726
47999CB00008B/2464